CW00343718

The River Jordan

The Way of Righteousness

M. Mubiana

The River Jordan

Copyright © 2014 M. Mubiana

ISBN-13: 978-0615952062

All rights reserved. Written permission must be secured from the publisher to use or reproduce any part of this book, except in the case of brief quotations embodied in the critical articles and reviews.

DEDICATION

This book is dedicated to Pastor Jamie and Sister Barbara Eitson for their forty years of church ministry at Park Heights Assembly in Tyler Texas. The revelation in this book came about after they invited me to speak at their ministry celebration. I am grateful to God for them and I give all the glory to God.

CONTENTS

ACKNOWLEDGMENTS

I thank my wife Jane K. Mubiana for praying for me and being supportive when I was writing this book. I am also grateful for all her support in ministry.

Chapter 1
The Word of God

The most important lesson in life is the lesson on the Word of God. When the Israelites were delivered from the house of bondage in Egypt, they went through the wilderness so that they could realize the importance of the Word of God. What God spoke in the beginning at creation came to pass and that is why what he speaks is always valid and dependable in every life situation.

Life really depends on what comes from the mouth of God. That word is what sustains and gives life to people. It is vitally important and necessary for people to depend on it. People must depend on it so that they can receive what God has promised. You and I today must depend on it to deal with life circumstances and then finally get to heaven.

The word of God basically reveals the will of God. It means we need it in order to navigate through life. Our sense of direction is erroneous, but God's direction is the right one and it is perfect. God will never go wrong because he is omniscient. He knows everything and when he makes a choice or decision, it is always right because he is aware of everything.

What does the Bible say about man? Well the Bible in Proverbs 14:12 says, "There is a way which seemeth right unto a man, but the end thereof are the ways of death" (KJV). Man can fall prey to deception, but not God. God knows the foundations of all mystical systems of sin and he is not subject to any of them. He is above all that is why we need to trust and depend on him. God knows that only his word can help us to get through any of our wilderness experiences.

In the book of Deuteronomy 8:3 in reference to Israel the Bible says, "And he humbled thee, and suffered thee to hunger, and fed thee with manna, which thou knewest not, neither did thy fathers know; that he might make thee know that man doth not live by bread only, but by every word that proceedeth out of the mouth of the Lord doth man live" (KJV). This was the best knowledge that anyone could acquire. The whole nation of Israel needed it and now every one of us still needs it. The word of God is important because it offers more than what natural food can offer.

Jesus had to go into the wilderness just like the nation of Israel did. In the wilderness, the people of God learnt how to live by every word that came out of the mouth of God. The importance of the word of God is usually realized as being helpful in difficulty times. When the word of God provides answers in those hard times God is glorified and people's lives are changed.

Jesus came in the flesh and experienced life as we do. The spirit of deception denies the fact that Jesus came in the flesh. In 2 John 1: 7 the Bible says, "For many deceivers are entered into the world, who confess not that Jesus Christ is come in the flesh. This is a deceiver and an antichrist" (KJV). Jesus was a human being just like every one of us. What happened to Israel also happened to Jesus.

Jesus was then supposed to come through the River Jordan to fulfill all righteousness. He acted his death and resurrection during his water baptism in the River Jordan. This was a prediction of what he would willingly do for mankind by the power of God. He had the power to lay down his life and take it back. Jesus' willingness to lay down his life for us in death was the act of obedience to God the Father.

In fact, righteousness is by faith through Jesus Christ. This was and is the will of God. In Hebrews 5:8, the Bible declares, "Though he were a Son, yet learned he obedience by the things which he suffered" (KJV). Jesus is the son of God and when he was in the wilderness fasting for fort days and nights he had to walk in obedience. His whole life was a life of obedience because he kept doing the will of God.

Remember that Israel was in the wilderness for

forty years before entering the land God promised Abraham. Jesus had to identify himself with Israel by going into the wilderness for forty days and nights. He obeyed the word of God and gained everything we all need and that is eternal life. He was not doing something different because he was fulfilling the plan God has for the chosen people.

When the word of God says that you are a chosen generation it means you are a special people of faith like the eight souls he saved during Noah's flood. In Christ, you are chosen by God just like Israel was chosen. During Noah's flood the rain fell for forty days and Jesus also fasted for forty days. This is how water baptism is really known to be from God. Eight souls in the Ark crossed over to the new world. It was a new beginning and in Christ we also crossover to a new beginning.

After Jesus came out from the wilderness, he began his ministry and in the process, chose twelve disciples he called apostles. Those twelve were not anywhere near perfection, but he chose them. He knew what would later come out of them. In John 6:70 the Bible says, "Jesus answered them, Have not I chosen you twelve, and one of you is a devil" (KJV). The fact is that Jesus chose the twelve apostles and nothing ever took him by surprise. The God of Abraham chose Israel, but the whole nation had to learn the importance of obedience to the word of God.

People without the knowledge of the word of God perish. In Hosea 4:6 the Bible says, "My people are destroyed for lack of knowledge: because thou hast rejected knowledge, I will also reject thee, that thou shalt be no priest to me: seeing thou hast forgotten the law of thy God, I will also forget thy children" (KJV). It is not a surprise after reading this Scripture that it becomes easy to notice that people who did not obey the word of God during the forty years in the wilderness died. Sin itself leads to a lot of suffering or even death.

Rejecting God's word means death and accepting it is life everlasting. Therefore, it matters that we should take God at his word so seriously. We should feed on it to make it in our spiritual journey. The word of God is what brings faith to us and through faith we make it in this wilderness of life.

The people who died in the wilderness during those forty years were full of unbelief. The word they heard did not mix together with faith. This means they did not consider the word of God as something they would apply to real situations in their lives. Those people had their own ways and they basically depended on systems that did not work. Since the word they heard did not mix with faith they lost out on the promise of God.

Today we are warned by the word of God not to be

like the people who did not have faith. In Hebrews 3:7-8 the Bible declares, "Wherefore (as the Holy Ghost saith, Today if ye will hear his voice, Harden not your hearts, as in the provocation, in the day of temptation in the wilderness" (KJV). The whole wilderness experience is like one day to The Lord. He refers to that experience as the day of temptation.

Your day of temptation can be that evil day the writer of the book of Ephesians talks about. All you can do is to be prepared for it and overcome by faith. Faith comes from what you hear from God and that is what really sustains you in your spiritual journey.

In Ephesians 6: 13 the Scripture says, "Wherefore take unto you the whole armour of God, that ye may be able to withstand in the evil day, and having done all, to stand" (KJV). We should do everything we can, to be able to stand in the evil day. The idea is that we should gain strength through the word of God to make sure we are prepared for this day of temptation.

God's plan is for us have to be strong through faith. In verse ten of the same chapter six of Ephesians the Bible says, "Finally, my brethren, be strong in the Lord, and in the power of his might" (KJV). Our strength is in the Lord and whatever we do we have to finally find ourselves standing strong in the lord. The Lord has provided resources so that we can be strong and these resources are found right in the word of God.

After Jesus fasted for forty days and nights in the wilderness the day of temptation also came. The first of all the temptation was about bread. This was relevant because Jesus had been fasting for all those days and nights. Although Jesus was physically weak and hungry the wilderness experience made him spiritually strong.

That is the reason why we have to be strong in the Lord because that is the only way we can overcome in that evil day. That was the same time Satan came to Jesus and tempted him. This was the evil day in the wilderness. That is why during temptations Jesus went by what the word of God declares. He quoted the word of God that was written and overcame.

This is how he activated the power of God against his adversary. What is written is forever established therefore no one can change it. This is the reason why the key is in knowing what the word of God says and then speaking it out against your presenting challenge. Whatever you do, choose to do what the word of God declares.

The best choice is to do what the word of God says because other alternatives offer wrong choices. Jesus chose you therefore you are the right choice. He chose not to turn stones into bread for the sake of just satisfying his physical hunger. He made the perfect choice and by choosing you he still made a perfect choice. You are chosen by Jesus Christ.

You are chosen by the one who makes perfect choices although he knows how weak you are. It is all because God can make something good out of you. You are chosen and you are special to him. As a matter of fact, you are chosen not because Jesus is going to benefit from you, but because you are going to benefit from him. In his ministry, Jesus did not take from people to sustain himself. Jesus knew that God was and is still the supplier in life therefore we should all overcome the temptation for personal gain when presented with such a temptation.

The apostle Paul in 2 Corinthians 2:17 says, "For we are not as many, which corrupt the word of God: but as of sincerity, but as of God, in the sight of God speak we in Christ" (KJV). This is one area that has trapped a lot of people. Paul said they were many who are peddling the word of God for personal gain. Jesus did not do it; Paul the Apostle did not do it therefore we should not do it too. The Lord will meet our needs according to his riches in glory.

God is also known as Jehovah Jireh, which means provider. God is our provider and this revelation came to Abraham in a most unique way. God asked Abraham to take his son and offer him as a sacrifice. How would you feel if someone asked you to give away something that you hold so dear to yourself? I believe you would probably wonder if you heard right and definitely not go with the idea. This is what happened to Abraham. God told Abraham to take the son he loves and offer him as a sacrifice. This must have been hard for Abraham, but since he was dealing with God, he knew God was able to resurrect his son if he had to offer him as a sacrifice.

Abraham depended on God. In Genesis 22:2 the Bible says, "And he said, Take now thy son, thine only son Isaac, whom thou lovest, and get thee into the land of Moriah; and offer him there for a burnt offering upon one of the mountains which I will tell thee of" (KJV). If there is something hard to do then this is one of them. It must have been hard to for Abraham to make a decision and obey God. When Abraham and his son Isaac were on the way to the top of the mountain, Isaac wondered about the whole process. He wondered how they carried everything they needed except the sacrifice itself.

At last he just had to ask his father. In Genesis 22: 7-8 the Bible says, "And Isaac spake unto Abraham his father, and said, My father: and he said, Here am I, my son. And he said, Behold the fire and the wood: but where is the lamb for a burnt offering? And Abraham said, My son, God will provide himself a lamb for a burnt offering: so they went both of them together" (KJV). Abraham did not say that Isaac was the sacrifice. He struggled with this idea from the very beginning of their journey to the mountain except he trusted that God was going to do something about it. Even if it meant raising his son after he was dead, he knew God would do it. We are not even sure if Sarah knew a lot about this whole situation, but God was in it.

However, when his son Isaac asked him about the sacrifice he spoke a prophetic word that has touched the human race and changed history forever. There was no room for sin therefore there was no room for lies. Abraham said, "God will provide himself a lamb for a burnt offering". Timing was everything to God and Abraham was willing to work with God. The fullness of time is what matters and in that time God provided a perfect sacrifice for humanity.

The sacrifice that God has provided is his own Son Jesus Christ. He died for the sins of the world and having faith in him makes you and me to become right with God. We become righteous because we have faith in Jesus Christ. Have faith in God and you will be his friend for eternity. When you are friends he will take care of you now and forever.

God provides for his people, but we have to learn how to activate his provision. We have to believe God like Abraham did. That is how he became righteous in the sight of God and God himself was very much pleased with him. The word of God that he heard created a challenge for him, but he just believed that God was able to deal with the situation. Abraham trusted God and we all need to trust God too.

In the day of temptation when Jesus looked at those stones he knew that turning them into bread was not really doing the will of God. Jesus obeyed God in that evil day in the wilderness by not turning stones in to bread. Obeying God is better than anything man can do for God. This same Jesus later turned water into wine; he surely could have turned stones into bread, but he did not. Why? Because he wanted to do the will of God. Jesus walked in obedience.

What is important in life is our redemption and it comes to us through Jesus Christ. If God wants anything, he provides for himself. When he does something, it means there is a good reason for it to be done. Turning stones into bread to satisfy his hunger would not have been the ideal thing during the day of temptation. That would have been a temporary solution outside the will of God.

Jesus did the will of God by refusing to turn stones into bread. According to Jesus, doing the will of God is like eating nutritious food. At Jacob's well at Sychar in Samaria Jesus talked about real food and real water. We all need that supply of eternal food and water.

In john 4: 31-32 the Bible says, "In the mean while his disciples prayed him, saying, Master, eat. But he said unto them, I have meat to eat that ye know not of" (KJV). The word of God is food indeed and the best way to benefit from it is not just by studying it, but by practicing it. This is the food the disciples did not know about. In verse thirty four of the same chapter the Bible says, "Jesus saith unto them, My meat is to do the will of him that sent me, and to finish his work" (KJV). Doing the will of God is food indeed.

Earlier before talking to the disciples when they came back from buying food, Jesus had talked to the Samaritan woman about the living water. Now, when Jesus was speaking to the Samaritan woman in John 4:14 he said and still says, "But whosoever drinketh of the water that I shall give him shall never thirst; but the water that I shall give him shall be in him a well of water springing up into everlasting life" (KJV). Jesus offers the living water and anyone willing can drink it and would never thirst again. This is something that really satisfies for eternity.

Now, we all need water and bread in the wilderness of this world. The true bread from heaven is Jesus Christ. In John 6:53 Jesus says, "... Verily, verily, I say unto you, Except ye eat the flesh of the Son of man, and drink his blood, ye have no life in you" (KJV). His flesh is real bread from heaven and his blood is real drink. When we eat his flesh and drink his blood we gain strength for our spiritual journey and it gives us hope that he will raise us up at the last day.

In verse fifty eight of the same chapter Jesus says, "This is that bread which came down from heaven: not as your fathers did eat manna, and are dead: he that eateth of this bread shall live for ever" (KJV). Jesus is the true bread from heaven. He is the word of God therefore receive him into your heart and you will not hunger or thirst anymore.

In John 1:1 the Bible says, "In the beginning was the Word, and the Word was with God, and the Word was God" (KJV). This is the Word that became flesh and that is Jesus Christ. In john 1:12 the Bible says, "But as many as received him, to them gave he power to become the sons of God, even to them that believe on his name" (KJV). When we receive Jesus Christ we receive eternal life. This means Jesus will raise us from the dead in the last day.

Chapter 2
Water Baptism

The experience that the nation of Israel had at the River Jordan was a miraculous one. It signified the death and resurrection of a people of God. God is talking to us about the death and resurrection experience that is required to go to heaven. Man's ability cannot accomplish this because it is the work of the Holy Spirit and water baptism symbolizes this experience really well.

In John 11: 25 Jesus Christ says, "...I am the resurrection, and the life: he that believeth in me, though he were dead, yet shall he live" (KJV). This is what faith in Christ can do. Faith can cause anyone to cross from death to life. Israel crossed the River Jordan by the help of God. Only God can do what was done for that chosen nation at that river. Since Jesus is the resurrection and the life, crossing over from death to life is done by the same power of God that helped Israel to cross the River Jordan. This is now supposed to be a personal experience in Christ and it means change.

When Israel was crossing the River Jordan, Joshua took twelve stones from the River Jordan's riverbed and placed them in Gilgal. These stones were used as a teaching aid for children so that they would know what

God did at the River Jordan by his supernatural power. In this way new generations in Israel would have faith.

Joshua also took twelve stones from the desert and placed them right in the channel where the river was flowing before the river was stopped. Joshua put the twelve stones on the riverbed. This shows us that the Israel that sinned died in the wilderness and the power of sin was a sure fact signified by this burial. When the stones were placed on the riverbed and the River Jordan began to flow, the stones were out of sight. When God takes away your sins, those sins are completely gone.

In this experience The Lord was saying that there is power that is so strong that it can raise stones to life. Stones have no life in themselves, but when the power of God touches them, they become alive. God gives eternal life and that life is from the river of living waters which is the river of God. This life is by the Holy Spirit and without the Holy Spirit there is no life.

During Noah's flood eight souls were saved and that was a form of baptism. When John the Baptist baptized people, he was doing the ministry that was from God. God was telling us that the way to the new life is through death and resurrection. Death has a real big part in the process of getting to God's promises. The promise of God is life itself. We must all cross from death to life and Jesus has made a way for us.

This is the only way to eternal life. The way to the Father is seen in what happened with Jesus at the River Jordan. When Jesus was being baptized by John the Baptist, John himself may not have had a complete revelation that Christ was supposed to died and resurrect from the dead for the human race. That is the reason why he did not want to baptize Jesus, but without Jesus being baptized, righteousness could not have come to us.

God's plan was to have Jesus come in the flesh to died and resurrect. This was not for himself, but for all humanity. Through Jesus we become the righteousness of God. That is the great exchange because he takes away our sins in exchange for his righteousness which comes to us by faith. Jonah was in the belly of a fish for three days and Jesus was in the deep dungeon of hell too. God allowed Jonah to see the light of day again. This was made possible by the resurrection power of God. God raised Jesus from the dead for us to see the true light of life. Let us not give up on this hope until we crossover to where life is eternal.

When Jesus talked about how he was going to go to Jerusalem to suffer and die, Peter took him aside and told him that something to that effect should not have to happen to him. Jesus rebuked Peter because his idea did not accommodate the plan of God for our redemption. Jesus knew the cross was the plan of God and that is why he was baptized by John in the River Jordan. In Matthew 16:23 the Bible says, "But he turned, and said unto Peter, Get thee behind me, Satan: thou art an offence unto me: for thou savourest not the things that be of God, but those that be of men" (KJV). The plan of God was centered on the Lord's death and resurrection.

John the Baptist witnessed this experience as it unfolded in the River Jordan by water baptism. That is what Christ himself referred to as the way of righteousness. In Matthew 3:15 the Bible says, "And Jesus answering said unto him, Suffer it to be so now: for thus it becometh us to fulfil all righteousness. Then he suffered him" (KJV). Jesus Christ was supposed to go through this process of redemption for the whole world. That is what Christ himself was talking to Peter about when he rebuked him. Water baptism was an example of what he would do for us in his death and resurrection. It was the plan of God.

It is Jesus who was supposed to die and resurrect so that we could all find eternal life. The key ingredient in the process is forgiveness. That is the reason why john baptized people because this was the baptism of repentance. People were turning away from sin that is why it is called the baptism of repentance. The human condition requires this experience. The River Jordan experience is the only way to God because everyone has sinned against him. Only Jesus has no sin. In Roman 3:

23 the Bible says, "For all have sinned, and come short of the glory of God" (KJV). You and I have sinned against God and without Christ we would all still remain sinners and that means being lost for eternity.

The people who were being baptized by John that time knew they were sinners. They went there seeking spiritual help. These people were honest with themselves as they sought for a relationship with God. They knew they were sinners and only God was able to forgive them. The fact is that only God was able to give them everlasting life.

We all have to be honest with God by acknowledging that we are sinners. The answer for our sinful condition is found in Jesus Christ. Everyone must believe in Jesus Christ for this experience to be a life giving experience. Faith is the key ingredient in the process and that is what helps people to receive the new birth experience from God.

Faith pleases God and it is the one and only way to the miraculous. In Mark chapter two, there is an account of a man who was sick. This man was paralyzed and the only thing his friends could do was to help him by the means of a stretcher. On this particular day his four friends carried him on his stretcher and brought him before Jesus in Capernaum.

That time Jesus was preaching in the house and a lot of people had gathered whereby it was not easy to go through the door because it was crowded. The crowd did not stop these men. These men went up the roof, made an opening and lowered their friend before Jesus. Imagine how difficult it was trying to get the paralyzed man onto the roof. These men were determined to help their friend and there was no way Jesus would have disappointed them.

Now, when Jesus saw that nothing successfully stopped them, he spoke some of the most gracious words that anyone can hear from God. In Mark 2:5 the Bibles declares, "When Jesus saw their faith, he said unto the sick of the palsy, Son, thy sins be forgiven thee" (KJV). When Jesus saw their faith he was pleased and he pronounce some of the most gracious words that anyone can hear. He said, "thy sins be forgiven thee".

This man's experience is a River Jordan experience because it is not just a death and resurrection experience; it is a great exchange that brings change to a limiting condition of sin. It is an experience about the forgiveness of sin. The River Jordan experience is saying that God identifies with you and you also identify with him. The River Jordan experience is saying that God has the final word in all our troubles.

Believers die with Jesus Christ and they resurrect with him. In Romans 8: 10-11 the Bible says, "And if Christ be in you, the body is dead because of sin; but the Spirit is life because of righteousness. But if the Spirit of him that raised up Jesus from the dead dwell in you, he that raised up Christ from the dead shall also quicken your mortal bodies by his Spirit that dwelleth in you" (KJV). Israel died in the wilderness because of sin just like our bodies must also die because of sin. However, we are quickened by the Spirit of God and that is the same Spirit that raised Christ from the dead.

The very same Spirit quickens our physical bodies. This means Jesus was fulfilling righteousness when he was being baptized by John in the River Jordan. In order for us to experience righteousness we need to die and rise with Christ. There was no sin in Christ when he was being baptized, but that was a provision for us to become righteous through faith. Without that fulfillment through Christ we cannot experience righteousness. Our righteousness is only through faith in Christ.

In Christ, we die to self and live to him. The twelve stones from the wilderness are buried forever and the other twelve stones from the river are a memorial. In Romans 6:4 the Bible says, "Therefore we are buried with him by baptism into death: that like as Christ was raised up from the dead by the glory of the Father, even so we also should walk in newness of life" (KJV). This is what makes our Christian life possible. The river Jordan experience is really what makes us free and it is rooted in our experience with Christ.

In the same chapter of Romans chapter six the Bible says that if anyone is dead it means he is free from sin. It means the people who came to John for water baptism at the River Jordan were expressing their desire for change. Yes, they were getting ready for the coming of Christ himself. They were getting ready for the one who would give them access to God and even baptize them into the Holy Spirit.

In order for us to experience righteousness we need to die and rise with Christ. The water baptism of Jesus Christ was a provision from God for us to become righteous through faith. Anyone who surrenders his life to God through Jesus becomes righteous since our righteousness is through faith in Christ.

Through Christ we die to self and live to him. The twelve stones are buried forever and the other twelve stones from the river are a memorial. This exchange is what makes our Christ like life possible. The River Jordan experience is what makes us free because of the faith we have in Christ. This is an experience with Christ.

In Romans chapter six the Bible says that if anyone

is dead it means he is free from sin. Does it mean that people in Christ are dead to sin that is why they can see God? Yes, because the Bible tells us that no man can see God and still remain alive. There must be the death experience to cross over and see God. No one can see God if he is not free from sin.

When people were being baptized in water, they were expressing their desire to be united to God with complete freedom from sin. Through this river Jordan experience, they had the opportunity to be free from sin so that they could be able to see God. This change occurs in those who turn away from sin and put their faith in Jesus Christ the son of God.

In John 8:36 Jesus says, "If the Son therefore shall make you free, ye shall be free indeed" (KJV). This freedom is due to the fact that he would die. There is no freedom without death. Water baptism is about the death of Christ and his resurrection. That is what gives us freedom from sin. Therefore, to be free from sin one has to identify with Christ in his death and resurrection.

Now, when we get baptized in water, we testify of that experience of his death and resurrection. It must first happen in our life and we only go through that physical experience of water baptism after the fact. We do not get baptized in water first because true change in anyone's life starts from the inside. We must first receive Jesus

Christ in our hearts and then get baptized in water.

The experience of getting baptized is for the fulfillment of righteous. Your faith in Christ makes that righteousness a reality. It is the will of God and it provides the way to the Father. Jesus took our sin and we took his righteousness. Without this experience we remain in death, but when we have this experience we have everlasting life. Water baptism then testifies to this fact that Christ has done this work and our lives change forever.

In the 2 Corinthians 5:17 the Bible declares, "Therefore if any man be in Christ, he is a new creature: old things are passed away; behold, all things are become new" (KJV). If you are in Christ it means you have had that separation from the past. The past and its carnal ways cannot keep you in bondage.

Your spirit becomes quickened by the Spirit of God and your passions change. In Christ, you value what God values and his life becomes your life. You become one with God and his desires become your desires. You then begin to feel the way God feels about people and that is how you end up becoming a vessel for good works in Christ.

The act of obedience to God will actually give us a sense of joy. When we disobey God, there will always be a sense of grief because the Spirit of God is grieved. In our Christian walk, we need to walk in obedience to God because that is what allows us to exercise our God given power over the powers of darkness.

Anyone who claims to be a Christian, but does not value obedience to God can never be effective at winning other people to Christ. Obedience to God has impact on people and it is a mighty force against the forces of darkness.

The experience of being one with God through the resurrection power of God in Christ is what makes this possible. What we do is to believe in Jesus Christ and our faith in him makes us to become one with him. We identify with him in water baptism and the reality happens in the spirit by the power of God.

Chapter 3
Spiritual Milestones

When Elisha crossed the River Jordan on dry ground; he experienced the power of God first hand. The parting of this river was no longer a religious story meant to raise the level of his faith in God. He probably heard about the twelve stones that were taken from the River Jordan when he was a child so many times, but his experience at the River Jordan with and without Elijah helped him to grasp the spiritual significance of that river of God.

In the past Elisha had heard about the power of God when Israel crossed this river. He really understood and knew for sure that it was the river of God. It was a fact that the people of God went through this river to inherit the land that God promised his friend Abraham. However, when Elisha crossed that River on dry ground, it became a reality. It was no longer just head knowledge. It was reality and that is what God wants us to experience in our relationship with him.

In the 80s as a young man I decided to live with some brothers in The Lord. We enjoyed our time together because of our devotion to The Lord. We had prayers every evening with a family that had prayers in their home every day. This was exciting for us and during that very time another brother in The Lord joined us. This brother read his Bible with unmistakable devotion although he had not yet received the gift of the Holy Spirit.

One day I went on a fast praying and asking the Lord for spiritual renewal. That Evening during our prayer meeting we prayed for this brother and he received the gift of the Holy Spirit. After this experience, he noticed something different when he read his Bible. One day he looked at his Bible and asked if that was the same Bible he always read. Well, we all knew for sure that it was the same Bible. What happened? This brother's experience with the Holy Spirit made the word of God so real and personal to him. The word of God now held new meaning to his life in a new way.

This new experience happened to this brother in The Lord and it also happened to Elisha. If this could happen to these people, it can also happen to you. When we experience God in a personal way, our taste for the word of God changes too. We end up relating to the things of God with a new intensity. All things become new and old things pass away.

In Acts 18: 24 the Bible says, "And a certain Jew named Apollos, born at Alexandria, an eloquent man, and mighty in the scriptures, came to Ephesus. This man was instructed in the way of the Lord; and being fervent in the spirit, he spake and taught diligently the things of the

Lord, knowing only the baptism of John" (KJV). This man went on to a new experience because God made a way for him. God wants all of us to get to new levels of experience with him.

In Matthew 11: 25 the Bible says, "At that time Jesus answered and said, I thank thee, O Father, Lord of heaven and earth, because thou hast hid these things from the wise and prudent, and hast revealed them unto babes" (KJV). There are smart people in this world who know a lot about things that have nothing to do with eternal life. God has not revealed these things to them because he chose not to. God has revealed them to people that Jesus called babies and that excited him.

Now, in Acts 18: 26 the Bible in reference to Apollos says, "And he began to speak boldly in the synagogue: whom when Aquila and Priscilla had heard, they took him unto them, and expounded unto him the way of God more perfectly" (KJV). God made a way for Apollos to get to that new level. Priscilla and Aquila explained to Apollos about other things that he did not know in regard to Christ. Jesus Christ has more in store for you and he has already made a way to take you to a new level. There is always more in Christ and his river never runs dry.

Do not settle for less than what God has for you. Hunger and thirsty for more of God and he will fill you. He will take you to new heights in life and ministry. God told Jeremiah the prophet to call on him because he would answer and show him great and mighty things. We can all now call on God through Jesus Christ and he will show us great and mighty things.

Chapter 4
The River Jordan Experience

Second Kings chapter two gives us an account of two people Elijah and Elisha and it clearly shows the significance of the River Jordan experience. The River Jordan for Israel separated the wilderness from the Promised Land. This is the reason why it offers a sense of separation from the past and people who experience this go through a real change in life.

In 2 Kings 2: 11-12 the Bible in reference to Elijah and Elisha says, "And it came to pass, as they still went on, and talked, that, behold, there appeared a chariot of fire, and horses of fire, and parted them both asunder; and Elijah went up by a whirlwind into heaven. And Elisha saw it, and he cried, My father, my father, the chariot of Israel, and the horsemen thereof. And he saw him no more: and he took hold of his own clothes, and rent them in two pieces" (KJV). The chariot was the chariot of fire and he horses where horses of fire. This was the true chariot of Israel and Elijah was bound for heaven. We all need to put our trust and hope in God.

When Elijah disappeared from sight, Elisha got hold of his mantle. Elisha took this mantle and went and stood on the River Jordan and called upon Elijah's God. He called upon God who has supernatural power. This was a time for action and Elisha was ready for it. In 2 Kings 2: 14 the Bible says, "And he took the mantle of Elijah that fell from him, and smote the waters, and said, Where is the Lord God of Elijah? and when he also had smitten the waters, they parted hither and thither: and Elisha went over" (KJV). This was the unfolding of an anointed ministry and the River Jordan was a significant part of it. Elisha's experience at the River Jordan led to the manifestation of God's anointing. Prayer was part of it because God hears prayer.

When a man has had the River Jordan experience he enters in to a new life. That new life has impact on what he does thereafter. The way opens up and God speaks by the way of miracles to magnify his Son Jesus Christ. Everything in ministry should be centered on lifting up Jesus Christ. Miracles should point to Jesus Christ as the way to the Father.

Elisha crossed the River Jordan on dry ground and that was a miracle. It was the way God made for him and that is how he went on to having a ministry that really impacted people's lives. When you crossover like Elisha did, you experience God's approval as the water of the Jordan miraculously separate. This is the way that God has ordained for all of us. We first have to find salvation before we can serve God. Jesus has made that possible for us by dying and rising from the dead. Jesus has made a way to the Father.

Elisha understood this mystery very well since he had that personal experience. No wonder a young lady who ended up in Naaman's house in Syria after the war knew about Elisha. The power of God was evident in Elisha's ministry and that is why the young lady recommended him for her master's healing. Her master Naaman was a captain in the army and had won many battles, but he had leprosy.

When he heard about Elisha he decided to visit the prophet for healing. When he visited, he had his own misconceptions just like all of us have misconceptions about how religious things should be done. When he arrived where the prophet Elisha lived, he expected him to come out and wave his hand over the infected spot on his body, but none of that happened. Elisha sent him to the River Jordan. The River Jordan is the river of God.

Elisha told him to go and dip himself in the river Jordan seven times. At first, he struggled with that idea, but finally chose to dip himself in the river. After he dipped himself in the river for the seventh time he was healed completely. In 2 Kings 5:14 the Bible says, "Then went he down, and dipped himself seven times in Jordan, according to the saying of the man of God: and his flesh came again like unto the flesh of a little child, and he was clean" (KJV). This was a great healing experience for Naaman. It is like a new birth experience and that is what God wants us to have before we can become co-heirs with Christ.

Many years earlier before what happened to Naaman; Israel came to the banks of The River Jordan and it was time for the crossing over experience. Joshua was told that he was going to be magnified at the crossing of the River Jordan. In Joshua 3:7 the Bible says, "And the Lord said unto Joshua, This day will I begin to magnify thee in the sight of all Israel, that they may know that, as I was with Moses, so I will be with thee" (KJV). God was with Joshua that day just as he promised.

After many years later, when Jesus was baptized in the River Jordan, the heavens opened up, God spoke with an audible voice and the Spirit of God lightened upon him as a dove. In Matthew 3:17 in regard to the Lord's baptism the Bible says, "And lo a voice from heaven, saying, This is my beloved Son, in whom I am well pleased" (KJV). On that day, God the Father magnified The Lord Jesus Christ. He was no longer just a son of Joseph the carpenter. He was the Son of the living God destined to redeem the human race, but had to go through the River Jordan experience.

Today we can now seek for more than just the "Elijah anointing" that was assumed to come in portions. Now we can seek for the same Holy Spirit anointing that was upon Jesus Christ. The River Jordan experience leads to the true authority of Christ over the powers of darkness. This is the time to take the Kingdom. Arise, be bold and proclaim the gospel of Jesus Christ because it is the power of God that leads to salvation.

God will always equip his people for the work ahead of them. Elijah did not abandon Elisha and that means God will definitely not abandon you too. God was with Elisha just as he was with Elijah.

One day Jesus looked at the disciples and told them that he was not going to leave them comfortless. He wanted to make sure they understood that he was going back to the Father and that they would do the same work he was doing without his physical presence. In John 14: 18 Jesus says, "I will not leave you comfortless: I will come to you" (KJV). Jesus knew how important the presence of God was to his disciples and he knows how important it is to you too.

In John 8:29 Jesus says, "And he that sent me is with me: the Father hath not left me alone; for I do always those things that please him (KJV). Although we know that faith is what pleases God, this statement points out that pleasing God has a lot to do with his presence. Jesus pleased God the Father and that ensured God's presence. This is the reason why every believer must experience the presence of God. The presence of the Holy Spirit is a fact and that is what makes the Lord's presence a reality. You and I must be well acquainted with the presence of God and the first step starts with our time alone with God in prayer.

After the Lord Jesus Christ was resurrected, he gathered his disciples together again and began to prepare them for his departure. He looked at them and reminded them of the promise of the Father. In Acts 1:4 - 5 the Bible says, "And, being assembled together with them, commanded them that they should not depart from Jerusalem, but wait for the promise of the Father, which, saith he, ye have heard of me. For John truly baptized with water; but ye shall be baptized with the Holy Ghost not many days hence" (KJV). At this time, the disciples were getting excited that may be Jesus was now going to restore the Kingdom to Israel and they asked him a question in those lines. Jesus instead revealed to them that their priority was to become witnesses and not worry about knowing the times or seasons that God has put in his power.

The truth of the matter is that we must have the River Jordan experience before we can be excited to talk about the end times. The plan of God will not mean a lot to us if we are not saved. Jesus does not want us to be preoccupied with the end of time discussions when we should be busy allowing the processes that make us become one with God and serve him better. You have to make sure you are saved and doing the work that God has set for you before being excited about the end times.

What Jesus wanted for the disciples was to be saved and then be effective at proclaiming the good news. This is the reason why in the book of Act 1:8 he says, "But ye shall receive power, after that the Holy Ghost is come upon you: and ye shall be witnesses unto me both in Jerusalem, and in all Judæa, and in Samaria, and unto the uttermost part of the earth" (KJV). This was like having that mantle that Elijah left for Elisha. The mantle was used in providing a way into the miraculous. We all need it because the harvest is plenty.

Without the Holy Spirit no miracle can manifest, which means the reality of being saved can not be realized, but by the Spirit of God. Every miracle that God does is by the Holy Spirit. This is the reason why Jesus promised the disciples that they were going to receive power after the Holy Spirit would come upon them. This is the same power that we all need for the work of the ministry.

After Jesus had the River Jordan experience that is when he began his ministry. Why did he wait for this experience? It is because he needed to be able to preach peace to Israel with power. In Acts 10:36-37 in regard to that preaching of that word of God by Jesus the Bible declares, "The word which God sent unto the children of Israel, preaching peace by Jesus Christ: (he is Lord of all:) That word, I say, ye know, which was published throughout all Judæa, and began from Galilee, after the baptism which John preached" (KJV). Peter was sharing this with the fellowship at Cornelius' house and the people who were present received the Holy Spirit.

In Acts 10: 38 Peter declared what happened to Jesus and says, "How God anointed Jesus of Nazareth with the Holy Ghost and with power: who went about doing good, and healing all that were oppressed of the devil; for God was with him" (KJV). After the River Jordan experience Jesus preached with power and not like the scribes. He opened blind eyes, healed the deaf, cleansed lepers, cast out demons and raised the dead because he was anointed with the Holy Spirit and Power.

Now, when the one hundred and twenty disciples who waited for the promise of the Father in the Upper room were filled with the Holy Spirit on the day of Pentecost, they received the power that Jesus wanted them to receive. This was like that mantle that Elijah left for Elisha. On that day, the disciples were equipped for service. On that same day, Peter preached to thousands of people who gathered on this day and warned them to turn away from the untoward generation and they repented

Thousands of people that same day gave their lives to Jesus. In Acts 2: 41 the Bible says, Then they that gladly received his word were baptized: and the same day there were added unto them about three thousand souls" (KJV). This is before the disciples performed any miracle and that many people were already giving their lives to Jesus Christ.

We all need to receive this power because that is what equips us as believers for service. Believers cannot do much without the Holy Spirit. What the Holy Spirit does in people's lives is what matters. He knows what people need and he will always meet their needs.

Chapter 5
The Call to the River of God

John the Baptist was calling people to the River Jordan so that they would be baptized. This baptism is the baptism of repentance which is a call for people to turn away from sin. The call to repentance is key in what God wants to accomplish through people.

No one can receive true forgiveness from God without responding to the call to repentance. John the Baptist told the people he was baptizing them in water, but there was someone who was coming after him and that is the one who was going to baptize people into the Holy Spirit. This implies that repentance is really a preparation for everything Jesus provides.

People need to turn away from sin before they can receive the Holy Spirit. The flame of the Holy Spirit can and will only burn in those who turn away from sin. This is the reason why John the Baptist was pointing the people to The Lord Jesus Christ because to get to Christ repentance was and is still a requirement. No one can receive the baptism in to the Holy Spirit without being saved first.

What is repentance? Repentance is a complete turnaround from a life of sin. Everyone who has ever repented has come to the realization that without God one is lost for eternity. Repentance starts with the realization that you are a sinner. People who think they are righteous since they attend church can never truly repent from sin. The true revelation of who we are without God is key in our turning away from the power of sin that keeps us in the bondage of sin.

There is no man who does not commit sin therefore every person needs to repent. No matter how good someone might feel about himself, he or she needs to turn away from sin. People keep sinning because of this power and it is a power that has kept the human race under its control for ages. The only solution to this situation is our Savior Jesus Christ. Anyone who calls on Jesus Christ receives forgiveness and that power of bondage gets broken.

John called people to the River Jordan so that they can experience the freedom that comes from knowing Jesus Christ. Jesus is the truth. He said that he is the way, the truth and the life. Since he is the truth, he sets people free. In John 8:32 he says, "And ye shall know the truth, and the truth shall make you free" (KJV). The truth provides true reality in life. In other words, truth is founded in reality. Anyone in this world can only be able to deal with any problem when reality is utilized and this is done by finding out the truth.

When Israel was crossing the River Jordan, Joshua instructed twelve men from each tribe to collect stones from the wilderness. Each one of those men took a stone from the wilderness and placed it in the middle of the River Jordan at the very exact spot where the priests who carried the Ark of the Covenant stood.

In Joshua 4: 9 the Bible says, "And Joshua set up twelve stones in the midst of Jordan, in the place where the feet of the priests which bare the ark of the covenant stood: and they are there unto this day" (KJV). These twelve stones were collected from the wilderness. Stones from the desert have sharp edges. If they are not well handle they can cut through anyone's skin. This is all because they have not gone through a river change process.

These stones represent the chosen people who came out of the house of bondage but perished in the wilderness because of unbelief. The word they heard did not mix with faith. They ended up not crossing the river Jordan into the Promised Land. Everyone who sinned in the wilderness never crossed into the Promised Land. Moses was only allowed to look at the land from a distance because he struck the rock instead of just speaking to it. Everyone who sinned in the wilderness perished in the wilderness.

Every believer goes through a wilderness experience. In this wilderness experience faith must be utilized to handle every overwhelming circumstance of life. Without faith, there can never be any hope.

Remember that all things are possible for everyone who believes. People who do not know how to use the power God has given to them cannot successfully take what he has promised. It takes a process to change a slave into a master. In the wilderness when the older people thought about the nice meals of Egypt, the younger generation only remembered bread from heaven called manna. At the crossing of the River Jordan those children who were now adults knew for sure that God was able to work a miracle again.

This was a generation that had seen miracle after miracle. Some of them saw how water gushed out of a rock and how manna fell from heaven. They saw how the Red sea parted and the whole nation crossed on dry ground. Once a young child sees the wall of sea water on the left and right side, his faith can never be in the wisdom of man, but in the power of God. This generation was ready to take the Promised Land when it crossed the River Jordan. It had the "can do spirit" and they took the land. You and I need to have the "I can do spirit" that is why we have to go through a process of change.

The next thing Joshua did was to instruct the twelve men to collect twelve stones from the river and placed them at the spot they were going to stay for the night after crossing. In Joshua 4:3 the Bible says, "And command ye them, saying, Take you hence out of the midst of Jordan, out of the place where the priests' feet stood firm, twelve stones, and ye shall carry them over with you, and leave them in the lodging place, where ye shall lodge this night" (KJV). The stones from the river are different from the stones taken from the wilderness.

Stones from the river have had to go through a change process. Their sharp edges are smoothed out. They have no sharp edges because they have had their river experience. These stones have had time to tumble and rolled along with the forces of the water in that river as it flowed for years.

Imaging how these stones started their journey the moment God spoke to Abraham about the promise. They went through that process for years until they were picked by the twelve men that Joshua instructed to pick them. The stones were in the river of God waiting to be picked and displayed. Their presence was meant to proclaim the works of God in Israel for generations.

You and I must go through that process too. God has to remove parts in our lives that do not reflect his image. He wants to take away things that hamper spiritual progress or obscure his image. This is a process that takes time, but it produces Christ like characteristics. God cannot use those who are not willing to go through this process. The river of God is flowing therefore flow with it. From glory to glory God is changing those who believe in Jesus Christ.

We are supposed to walk in the Spirit so that we do not fulfill the desires of the flesh. The desires of the flesh are like sharp edges of the stones picked from the wilderness. They can end up hurting other people in subtle ways. When a believer walks in the spirit he begins to produce certain characteristics that are a product of the Spirit of God.

In Galatians 5:16 the Bible says, "This I say then, Walk in the Spirit, and ye shall not fulfil the lust of the flesh" (KJV). This is the crossover process and it is done by walking in the Spirit. As you walk with The Lord people will notice the change. This is how believers in Christ ended up be being called Christians in Antioch. They exemplified the life of Christ. This life was and is only possible by the Holy Spirit.

When you walk with God in this manner you will discover that certain characteristics the Bible calls fruit will manifest in your life. The fruit of the Spirit is a product from the river of God. If the Spirit of God dwells in you then you will produce fruit as you yield to him.

There came a time in Israel when it had not rained for years and Elijah was the prophet. The people had turned away from The Lord, but Elijah was determined to bring them back to God. Elijah preached repentance and he was effective at his work as a prophet. The anointing on his life is what was recognized as the Spirit of Elijah.

The same Spirit of Elijah was on John the Baptist as he preached repentance at the River Jordan. The same anointing moved Elijah to preach against the prophets of

Baal. In 1Kings 18:31-32 the Bible says, "And Elijah took twelve stones, according to the number of the tribes of the sons of Jacob, unto whom the word of the Lord came, saying, Israel shall be thy name: And with the stones he built an altar in the name of the Lord : and he made a trench about the altar, as great as would contain two measures of seed" (KJV). After Elijah prepared the altar that is when he challenged the prophets of Baal. That day Elijah prayed to God and God answered his prayer by fire. Fire came from heaven and consumed the sacrifice and people fell on their faces and turned back to God.

When John the Baptist preached repentance, people confessed their sins and brought forth fruit meet for repentance. The Spirit of Elijah was upon him because he was filled with the Holy Spirit from his mother's womb. What people knew was that Elijah was to come first before everything would be restored in Israel.

One day Jesus took three of his disciples on a high mountain and became transfigured before them. Suddenly Moses and Elijah also appeared and they were talking about the work of redemption that he was about do for the human race. The experience on the mountain was so good that they just wanted to stay there for a long time. However, after they saw the cloud and heard the voice of God the Father everything reverted to the natural.

This sparked a question about the coming of Elijah that they heard of from the scribes. In Matthew 17: 10-12 the Bible says, "And his disciples asked him, saying, Why then say the scribes that Elias must first come? And Jesus answered and said unto them, Elias truly shall first come, and restore all things. But I say unto you, That Elias is come already, and they knew him not, but have done unto him whatsoever they listed. Likewise shall also the Son of man suffer of them" (KJV). Jesus clearly pointed out that John the Baptist was the one who would come and they did not know that he was the Elijah they were waiting for.

Jesus explained further that the same thing was also going to happen to him because they would not know that he was the Messiah. This is the reason why they crucified him too. Jesus Christ is the king of glory and for him to have been crucified means those who did it were ignorant. When he was on the cross he asked God the Father to forgive them because they did not know what they were doing. They could not have crucified the king of glory if they knew him. The Bible in 2 Corinthians 3:15 says, "But even unto this day, when Moses is read, the vail is upon their heart" (KJV).

In Acts 17:30 the Bible says, "And the times of this ignorance God winked at; but now commandeth all men everywhere to repent" (KJV). Jesus overlooks ignorance. He wants every one's life to turn around for the better. Repentance is a complete turnaround from sin. This is what John the Baptist preached and it is what we are supposed to preach. God is ready to forgive anyone who turns to him no matter how filthy he or she might feel. God's forgiveness is available for everyone today.

In 1 John 1:9 the Bible says, "If we confess our sins, he is faithful and just to forgive us our sins, and to cleanse us from all unrighteousness" (KJV). God is faithful and will forgive you when you ask for forgiveness. The whole process leads to a lot of change in life. God is also just; therefore, there is nothing unjust that will go unpunished. God will take care of you if you submit yourself to him.

Chapter 6
God's Approval

When Jesus told the disciples to wait for the promise of the father he wanted to equip them for service as he was also equipped. Jesus wanted them to bring glory to God therefore they had to be introduced to the one who manifests miracles here on earth and that is the Holy Spirit. The law of the spirit had to take over and the law of sin and death had to pass away so that they would be witnesses. This was a new beginning.

In Joshua 1: 2 the Bible says, "Moses my servant is dead; now therefore arise, go over this Jordan, thou, and this entire people, unto the land which I do give" (KJV). This command came to Joshua because God chose him to lead the people across the Jordan River into the Promised Land. What God had promised for Israel came by the river of God. The promises of God come to us through Christ and in him there in a river of life. That is the river of God.

The whole nation of Israel at that time knew Joshua as an assistant to Moses, but was he fit for the next job? That might have been the question that was going through their minds. Due to all this, God had to come through for Joshua. God spoke to Joshua and prepared him for his new responsibilities. God had to show the whole nation that his seal of approval was on Joshua.

In Joshua 3:7 the Bible says, "And the Lord said unto Joshua, This day will I begin to magnify thee in the sight of all Israel, that they may know that, as I was with Moses, so I will be with thee" (KJV). When the people knew that God had approved Joshua they had no problems submitting to his leadership.

People have no problem following a ministry leader who is approved by God. In the case of Joshua, a great wonder was done so that the people could know that God had approved him as a leader in Israel. God parted the River Jordan and Israel crossed into the Promised Land. God was dealing with Israel so that the whole nation could be of one mind and heart. That is how they managed to cross the River Jordan.

There are people in your life who will always think of you as someone who is not set out for great things. The reality is that God has to approve you first before anyone can ever think that you can do what God has set out for you to do. Listen to God because he will always take you into a new dimension of victory in your seasons of life. This is a place you have never been to before and it is more like each and every new day that you anticipate. Only God has been there before you since he knows the end from the beginning. Your best friend has never been to that place and that is why his or her advice may not be as useful.

Who do you listen to then? Well, listen to those who walk with God and really care about you. If your pastor hears from God and cares about your spiritual needs he will then watch over you. Always allow yourself to be in agreement with God in every way possible so that you can serve him more effectively. What matters is that spiritual connection with God.

Have you ever tried to share with a friend about some venture you are about to take and ended up having your plans or ideas stripped down to nothing? A friend cannot see things as perfect as God sees them. What God speaks to you in private will always be confirmed in the open. What God speaks comes to pass no matter how the circumstances might appear like. However, remember not to sabotage whatever he says by the way you think or speak. Agree with God because that is what Mary did when she responded to the Angel's message about the conception of Jesus. Mary was willing for things to be done according to the message from God.

Faith is about things you hope for; therefore, you may have to expect to wait for a period of time and that experience requires patience. In Galatians 4: 4 the Bible says, "But when the fulness of the time was come, God sent forth his Son, made of a woman, made under the law" (KJV). God comes through at the right time. God is

never early or too late; he is always on time. During that
waiting period fix your eyes on Jesus because the
promises of God always come to pass.

This is the reason why Israel walked around the
city of Jericho for the whole week without uttering a
word. It is easy to talk yourself out of your victory by
what you say to yourself. Let the word of God have full
impact by taking God at his God. That is faith and it
pleases God. Obedience in those times of silence will
prove profitable later. That is why faith has that element
of hope. Faith sees the invisible and acquires the peace
that passes all understanding to keep the mind at rest.

When Israel was about to cross the River Jordan
Moses had just died. If you have ever led a team on a
mission trip you will always hear this question from team
members, what do we do now? Most likely a good
number of people in Israel were asking this same
question. Moses was dead, now what were they supposed
to do? If you suggested to them that someone like Joshua
was going to takeover, they would have probably laughed
you to scorn because to some of them this was just an
assistant.

They never saw him perform any miracle like
Moses. That picture as an assistant to Moses just does not
fade so easily. That is the reason why God came on the
scene and introduced Joshua to his people with a seal of
approval. The River Jordan was divided as according to

the plan of God and Joshua received the respect that God wanted him to have.

There were people who looked at Jesus and thought that he was nothing, but the son of Joseph the carpenter. These people had so much familiarity with Jesus that they never allowed themselves to see greatness in him. In Matthew 13: 54-55 the Bible says, "And when he was come into his own country, he taught them in their synagogue, insomuch that they were astonished, and said, Whence hath this man this wisdom, and these mighty works? Is not this the carpenter's son? is not his mother called Mary? and his brethren, James, and Joses, and Simon, and Judas" (KJV). Due to this attitude Jesus just did a few miracles because they did not have faith. They did not have confidence in him because they thought to themselves nobody among them is meant for great things.

In 2 Timothy 2: 15, 16 the Bible says, "Study to shew thyself approved unto God, a workman that needeth not to be ashamed, rightly dividing the word of truth. But shun profane and vain babblings: for they will increase unto more ungodliness" (KJV) God's approval is vitally important in ministry because it is a way God proves that you are supposed to be doing what he has appointed for you to do. Avoid group pressure that would force you to abandon things that really matter. The works of God in your ministry or life are God's approval and they speak to the skeptics. Let God speak on your behalf.

Group pressure has been a source of defeat for unheard visionaries. Do not allow the self-defeating attitudes of other people kill your vision. God sets your possibilities and all you have to do is to obey his word. Have the fear of God and believe that you can do what God has set for you to do. Go and fly were the eagles soar above the mountains of life. You are more than an eagle because your strength is from God. Go mount up with wings as an eagle, for now is your time.

If you were to test the group of people you belong to, just announce to them that you want to buy a new luxury car or just something they think is out of their reach and you will find out what they think about themselves. Some of them might take you aside and advise you that such a car or that particular thing you want to have is very expensive you cannot afford it. It is like they have set limits for themselves and they expect you to go by those same limits. They assume you are not different from them.

Groups that people belong to or identify with will always have a limiting belief system. There is always a certain level of unbelief that will be present in most groups. This shows that unbelief has confined them and their thinking is shackled in chains of the so called "you cannot do this or that" kind of life. If you are in Christ you can do all things that Christ wants you to do.

What these people have in mind might point to anything like a car, house, boat or that particular thing you want as only being possible for those other people on the affluent side of the city and not for you. Remember that whatever belongs to God is yours and everything on earth belongs to God. That is how rich you are, but you will always use what you need at the time you need it.

Things have to change because when God created the world, he gave you everything in it in abundance. There is plenty of water, air and sunlight for you and everyone else. Everything is plentiful except those things that involve human systems. Why? Man is generally stingy, but God is generous and he has generously given you everything you need. When God is pleased, there is nothing to worry about because he will come through for you. Have faith in God because having faith puts him in the first place among all other things you desire.

Now, God made sure the people had respect for Joshua. That Hebrew name Joshua means Jesus. God was pointing Israel at the crossing of the Jordan River to Jesus who would save his people from sin. Now the true Joshua who is Jesus has made a way for us to crossover to the eternal promises of God. Through his body, he has made a way for us to go into the presence of God.

When Jesus came back from the wilderness after fasting for forty days and nights he came with the authority of God. He spoke as one who had authority and not as the scribes. He healed the sick, cleansed lepers, restored sight to the blind, cast out demons and raised the dead. God was magnifying Jesus Christ. The miracles he did testified to the fact that God had approved him.

When he was training those apostles, God the Father came in a cloud on a high mountain and told them who Jesus was and that they should listen to him. God magnified Jesus and he has continued to magnify him from generation to generation by miracles through the hands of those he has sent to preach the gospel. If there is someone to listen to, then listen to the word of God because that word is Jesus Christ the son of the living God.

Jesus has now entered the holy of holies and has presented his blood which speaks a better word of reconciliation through the forgiveness of sin. The blood of Abel cried to God when his brother Cain killed him, but he was not as perfect as Jesus is. The blood of Jesus now speaks a better word than that of Abel or any animal because it speaks the word of forgiveness. When Jesus forgave a sick man, his forgiveness was confirmed by healing. His forgiveness opens a way into the miraculous. Surely his forgiveness takes us into the promises that no man can take away from us.

This is what continues to bring people to God. In John 12: 32 Jesus says, "And I, if I be lifted up from the earth, will draw all men unto me" (KJV). You may wonder, did he not draw people to himself as multitudes gathered in the thousand around him? He did draw multitudes, but what he is talking about now includes crossing over into heaven itself. This means people would have to come to God and find eternal life because he would conquer death.

The resurrection of Jesus Christ is key in gathering the harvest of souls in this world. It is the only way to God the father and Jesus is the only one who could do that special kind of work. This makes Jesus Christ the only way to God. The River Jordan experience is central to what God has in store for his people. It is a crossover place into the impossible.

This is a place where people that God uses crossover to what he has assigned them to have and do. The Lord's assignment was beginning at the River Jordan, but like Elisha with a mantle there was a need for the Holy Ghost and fire baptism. This is the reason why Jesus told the disciples to wait for when he ascended to the Father in heaven. The chariot of fire took Elijah and now we all need the fire that comes from heaven for us to truly populate heaven.

In John 10: 25 in response to those who questioned Jesus authority the Bible says, "Jesus answered them, I told you, and ye believed not: the works that I do in my Father's name, they bear witness of me" (KJV). The works of God are done by the Holy Spirit and they are a powerful witness of who Christ is. This is the same Spirit that those who believe in Jesus are led by so as to manifest the works of God. The works of God are what shows God's approval.

It is better to be like Mary who responded to the message from the Angel by accepting it saying that it should be so according to what was spoken to her. That is faith and it is the only thing that pleases God. Contrast that to Zacharias experience with an Angel. Since he did not believe the good news that the Angel brought, he was not allowed to speak until the promise was fulfilled. This is like Israel's match around Jericho that was done in silence until the day the walls of that fortified city came tumbling down.

In Luke 1:20 the Angel Gabriel told Zacharias, "And, behold, thou shalt be dumb, and not able to speak, until the day that these things shall be performed, because thou believest not my words, which shall be fulfilled in their season" (KJV). Have faith in God no matter what comes your way. Whether you are a preacher or not, you will see wonders if you have faith in God.

Now again, at the River Jordan God said that he was pleased with Jesus (Yeshua or Joshua). This is clearly stated in Matthew 3:16, 17 where the Bible says, "And Jesus, when he was baptized, went up straightway out of the water: and, lo, the heavens were opened unto him, and he saw the Spirit of God descending like a dove, and lighting upon him: And lo a voice from heaven, saying, This is my beloved Son, in whom I am well pleased" (KJV). At the River Jordan God again magnified Joshua and who is Jesus to us in this generation. The heavens opened up and God said that he was pleased with Jesus Christ. This was a miracle because the heaven opened and God spoke in the presence of those who attended the baptism service that day.

This wonder happened once and it will never happen again. God set a seal of approval on Jesus Christ and the people knew he was sent from God. It was like the time when God told Joshua that he was going to magnify him at the crossing of the River Jordan. The name Joshua in Hebrew is the name Jesus. This name proclaims salvation from sin that is why people were confessing their sins as John the Baptist was baptizing them in water. Jesus saves people from sin.

Chapter 7
The Word of Faith

The word of God is dependable and that is why it remains the source of faith. In Romans 10: 17 the Bible says, "So then faith cometh by hearing, and hearing by the word of God" (KJV). Faith is more than just identifying with a religious group. The source of faith is not religious beliefs. Having faith in religious ideology produces practices that can seem to resemble faith when it is not. There is only one true faith and that is faith in the true God the creator of heaven and earth.

True faith is established on something that can never be shaken. It is established on something stable and strong. The psalmist compares something like that to a rock that is higher than him. In Psalms 61: 2 the Bible says, "From the end of the earth will I cry unto thee, when my heart is overwhelmed: lead me to the rock that is higher than I" (KJV). There is a rock that is higher and it is rooted in God himself.

In John 1:1 the Bible says, "In the beginning was the Word, and the Word was with God, and the Word was God" (KJV). This Word is the very source of our faith. In verse fourteen of the same chapter we are told, "And the Word was made flesh, and dwelt among us, (and we beheld his glory, the glory as of the only begotten of the Father,) full of grace and truth" (KJV). Jesus is the Word that was with God and was God. We are told that he was God. Does it mean he stopped being God? Well, the Scripture clearly states that he came in the flesh. We are told that the Word was made flesh.

Now, every teaching that does not accept this fact is then false. In 1 John 4: 2 the Bible declares, "Hereby know ye the Spirit of God: Every spirit that confesseth that Jesus Christ is come in the flesh is of God" (KJV). When Jesus walked on the face of the earth he was a man.

When a ruler called him Good Master he made it clear that only God was good. In Luke 18: 19 the Bible says, "And Jesus said unto him, Why callest thou me good? none is good, save one, that is, God" (KJV). The word "God" is supposed to refer to him as the one who has supernatural power. He is the only one who is perfect in every area. That is why he is the source of our faith. What he speaks is dependable and no one can counsel him on any issue. He is God and when you have faith in him, you have faith in the true rock of ages.

Life has real life problems therefore you need someone bigger and stronger to deal with them. Only faith in the omnipotent God can do this. The worst enemy to man is death and without the help of God man is defeated and lost without hope. Only God has the ability to raise any man from the dead. God has that power and our faith in him creates a way to the impossible. If anyone claims to be God, but has no ability to raise someone from the dead such a one is not God. No man on earth is God.

The God of Jesus Christ is God indeed and death has no power over him. He is the true and only God and he is the one who raised Jesus Christ from the dead. Jesus was God who became man. He is that Word that became flesh and in his days as a man he spoke to troubling life issues and the power of God manifested powerful results. This was all because Jesus was anointed and that is what made his ministry more effective. There are things in this world that obey nothing, but the Word of God.

When Jesus was in a storm with his disciples he spoke to the storm. He commanded demon spirits to come out of people who were vexed by demon power and they were set free. The word that Jesus spoke was with power. This does not mean his voice was loud to signify power. Power refers to the ability to perform extraordinary things.

Jesus spoke and things happened just like the prophetic word in Isaiah 55: 11 which says, "So shall my word be that goeth forth out of my mouth: it shall not return unto me void, but it shall accomplish that which I please, and it shall prosper in the thing whereto I sent it" (KJV). God sent the living Word who is Jesus Christ to us. He was a man having flesh and blood like us, but he did God's will and successfully accomplished God's purpose in this world.

Jesus was sent into the world by God and he did and is still doing what the Father sent him here to do. When he came, he was a man just like all of us. It would not have been right for God to demand so much of us if he did not supply the resources. He sent The Lord Jesus Christ and equipped him for the task. Jesus also sent the disciples with the same supernatural ability that comes from God which is the same anointing that was on Jesus Christ. The same anointing equips believers for service today.

In John 17: 18 Jesus Christ prayed and said, "As thou hast sent me into the world, even so have I also sent them into the world" (KJV). The same anointing that calmed storm, dried up a fig tree, turned water in wine, healed the sick, set the demon possessed free and raised the dead is for us. This anointing of power is not for show so that we can claim we are great men and women of power. This power is for ministry to those in need and both the poor and rich in this world have needs.

When Jesus began his ministry, he was first baptized in the River Jordan. This was symbolic of what God by his power would do for the human race. God sent his Word into this world to bring deliverance from the power of death. In Hebrews 2:14-15 the Bible declares,

"Forasmuch then as the children are partakers of flesh and blood, he also himself likewise took part of the same; that through death he might destroy him that had the power of death, that is, the devil; And deliver them who through fear of death were all their lifetime subject to bondage" (KJV). Life time bondage has now been removed because of what Jesus did for us. Jesus conquered death and has delivered us from its power. All what you and I have to do is to believe in Christ to overcome the enemy of men's souls.

This Jesus is the Word of God and he was sent to accomplish God's purpose on earth. In Psalms 107:20 the Bible says, "He sent his word, and healed them, and delivered them from their destructions" (KJV). The Word of God was sent from heaven and its purpose was accomplished. Jesus did not go back to heaven empty handed. He took the blood he shed on that cross of Calvary and presented it in the Holy of Holies as our high priest. The blood was accepted in heaven and the Holy Spirit was sent to us. God has delivered us with a great deliverance. The deliverance in Egypt for the nation of Israel was great, but this one is even greater.

Jesus is the Living Word who died on that cross of Calvary that Friday afternoon outside of Jerusalem. They took his body and laid it in the tomb and was there that night. On Saturday everyone in Jerusalem was busy being as religious as can be by keeping the Sabbath. What happened to Jesus? Did he stop to exist? Not at all.

His body still laid there on Saturday night and that Sunday morning he was walking among the living again. Jesus is the Living Word. In 1 Peter 3: 19 the Bible in reference to Jesus after his death says, "By which also he went and preached unto the spirits in prison" (KJV). He went into the deep dark dungeons of hades and preached to those who were lost in Noah's flood. This unfolds the mystery of water baptism.

The Bible tells us that Jesus preached to the spirits in prison. On earth Jesus' body was in the tomb, but in the spirit world he was preaching the word of faith to the spirits. In 1 Peter 3: 20- 21 the Bible refers to the spirits and says, "Which sometime were disobedient, when once the longsuffering of God waited in the days of Noah, while the ark was a preparing, wherein few, that is, eight souls were saved by water. The like figure whereunto even baptism doth also now save us (not the putting away of the filth of the flesh, but the answer of a good conscience toward God,) by the resurrection of Jesus Christ" (KJV). When The Lord's body was in the tomb, the forces of evil thought the Living Word of God was finally conquered, but before that Sunday morning he was the only light in that deep dungeon of death.

On that third day Jesus arose and defeated death and water baptism proclaimed that ever since John began baptizing in the river Jordan. The Lord Jesus' death and resurrection is the reality of what water baptism symbolizes and now it is the way we identify with him.

The work of the Holy Spirit in our lives is what really makes this a reality during and after the new birth experience.

In John 1:5 the Bible says, "And the light shineth in darkness; and the darkness comprehended it not" (KJV). Jesus is the light and wherever he is he prevails against darkness. In hell, the powers of darkness could not prevail against him. That Sunday morning, Jesus arose from the dead and restored the authority that God gave to man when he first created him. Man can now have eternal life.

Jesus walked out of those dungeons with the victory that no one can fathom. He arose from the dead and now has the keys of the kingdom of God. In Revelation 1: 18 the resurrected Jesus says, "I am he that liveth, and was dead; and, behold, I am alive for evermore, Amen; and have the keys of hell and of death" (KJV). Jesus is alive and he is seated at the right hand of God the Father in heaven. He accomplished what God sent   him to do.

After his resurrection in John 20:21 the Bible says, "Then said Jesus to them again, Peace be unto you: as my Father hath sent me, even so send I you" (KJV). All believers are sent by Jesus Christ and their authority is legitimately given to them by God. John the Baptist's authority was from God, Jesus' authority is from God and your authority as a believer is from God through

Jesus Christ. Spread the word of faith without reservation or fear for the Lord your God is with you.

When Jesus was baptized in the river Jordan by John the Baptist he was stating that he was going to die and resurrect in order to defeat death. Death is man's worst enemy therefore the death and resurrection of Jesus Christ defeated man's worst enemy. This was God's plan of Salvation for mankind. During Noah's flood the first souls were saved from death and that pointed to water baptism. Later Joshua crossed the River Jordan with a new nation of Israel. Those who did not mix the Word of God with faith perished in the wilderness and those who had faith crossed into the Promised Land.

Baptism is for crossing over from death to life. Even when the word of God decrees that everyone must die because of sin, baptism makes the way. The way is the way of righteousness and Jesus fulfilled the way of righteousness at the river Jordan by being baptized in water. The Bible tells us that the wages of sin is death and since all of us have sinned we all deserve to die. However, through Jesus Christ and because of his death and resurrection we now crossover to eternal life. Now when you have faith in Christ you pass from death to life.

In Hebrews 4:2 the Bible in reference to the children of Israel and us today says, "For unto us was the gospel preached, as well as unto them: but the word preached did not profit them, not being mixed with faith

in them that heard it" (KJV). The Word of God that we
hear today must mix with faith. It is the word of faith
because it is the Word of God. The word of faith will see
you through every life situation and grant you access to
the promises of God. This is what makes man to
crossover to eternal things. Faith has in the past helped
the people of God in real life problems and now the issue
of death has been dealt with successfully though Jesus
Christ. If you are in Christ the Bible says that you have
already crossed from death to life.

Faith is what makes you become aware of the
things that are invisible to the physical eye. Not only that,
but it is also the manifestation of trust or confidence in
the power of God. This is how our lives get changed by
the Spirit of God. We now have access to the power of
God because of what Christ has done for us. Our lives
can now manifest that same life that was in Christ.
Christ's life is the light of all men. When you have Christ
in your life, you have life and that life is the light of all
men.

Chapter 8
The Temple Curtain

The way into the presence of God has now opened up for all of us. However, we have to believe in Jesus to make it to the other side. The other side is only being prepared for those who believe in Jesus Christ.

Jesus is the only way to God the Father in heaven. There is no other way, but Jesus. It is surprising that a lot of people find this fact hard to comprehend.

Some people try to argue that there are many other ways to God. If anyone claims that he is using another way to God then such a one must prove how that is factual. Jesus proved he is the way because he died and rose again. This is the way that was proclaimed by God for ages. This way is the way of righteousness and that means the way of faith. That is the same way Jesus himself had to fulfill when he was baptized by John the Baptist in the River Jordan.

The way to God the Father in heaven is through faith in Christ. That is the way that God has set up so that we can all be justified when we come to Jesus for forgiveness of our sins. That is the way of righteousness. Good religious works before God cannot lead anyone to God in heaven. Faith in Christ is the only way to heaven.

There is no human need or problem too big for God to meet when faith is present. This is what gives us hope that we will walk the streets of gold in heaven and worship God who is full of mercy for eternity. In John 14: 5 the Bibles says, "Thomas saith unto him, Lord, we know not whither thou goest; and how can we know the way (KJV). The question Thomas asked is still a valid question today. How do we know the way to God?

According to the answer that Jesus gave, the way is not a concept. It is not a well conceptualized idea. Ideas will never take anyone to heaven. It is a person who will do it and that person is Jesus Christ. In John 14: 6 the Bible says, "Jesus saith unto him, I am the way, the truth, and the life: no man cometh unto the Father, but by me" (KJV). Jesus has that authority of letting people to go to heaven.

There is no thought, ideology or philosophical idea that can take people to heaven. Thoughts, concepts and ideologies are temporary, but the Spirit of God is eternal. It has to be the Spirit of God who does that kind of work and through Jesus the work has been done.

On the cross Jesus said that it was finished. It is finished therefore we can now have access to what God has promised. Jesus is the way and he has gone before us already. Faith is what turns anything impossible into something possible and that is how the way to God the Father becomes a reality.

When Jesus rebuked people who were selling and buying in the temple in Jerusalem for turning the place of worship into a market place, he pointed out that he was going to build the temple not made by human hands. In John 2: 18-19 the Bible says, "Then answered the Jews and said unto him, What sign shewest thou unto us, seeing that thou doest these things? Jesus answered and said unto them, Destroy this temple, and in three days I will raise it up" (KJV). Jesus was referring to his physical body because that was the place the Holy Spirit of God dwelt.

Sin brings destruction and Jesus was pointing out that he was going to destroy that temple and build it in three days. Jesus was referring to his death and resurrection. It is the Spirit of God who builds the temple of God. In Psalm 127:1 the Bible declares, "Except the Lord build the house, they labour in vain that build it..." (KJV). Man cannot really build the house of God because only God builds it.

The human condition of sin is what led to the destruction of the body of Jesus Christ. When he hang on that cross it was for our sin. He had no sin, but when he hang on that cross he became sin for us and through that we can now become the righteousness of God. Identifying with him in his death and resurrection makes this personal and possible. This is what water baptism symbolizes. In Hebrews 10: 20 the Bible says, "By a new and living way, which he hath consecrated for us, through the veil, that is to say, his flesh" (KJV). When the Bible says his flesh it refers to his body and that is the veil.

Moses built the tabernacle according to the pattern that was revealed to him. Every part of the building carried some meaning. The veil separated the holy place from the holy of holies. The Ark of the Covenant was in the holy of holies and the table of bread, the lamp and the altar of incense was in the holy place. No one was allowed to go into the Holy of Holies except the high priest and that was done once every year on the Day of Atonement.

When the high priest went in to the holy of holies he sprinkled the blood of animals onto the mercy seat located between the angelic beings. This high priest did this for years, but the veil still remained intact because the way was not open for the human race to go into heaven itself. When Jesus died for us, he ascended to heaven and presented the blood he shed at Calvary to God.

That blood is the blood of the New Testament and it speaks a word of forgiveness to God on our behalf. The word it speaks to God is a better word. In Hebrews 12:24 the Bible says, "And to Jesus the mediator of the new covenant, and to the blood of sprinkling, that speaketh better things than that of Abel" (KJV). The blood of animals could not take away our sins, but the blood of Jesus takes away every sin.

The Bible says that if we confess our sins he is faithful and just to forgive us our sins. He is just, in the sense that he cannot forgive one person and not forgive another for the same sin. He does not show any kind of partiality. He is faithful and just therefore he will not overlook your situation.

This is how the way to God has been made and it is the way of righteousness because it provides sanctification for those who put their faith in Jesus Christ. In Hebrews 10:10 the Scripture says, "By the which will we are sanctified through the offering of the body of Jesus Christ once for all" (KJV). The body of Christ is the veil that has now opened the way to God for us.

When the temple which is the body of Christ was offered on the cross the way opened for us. In Mark 15:37-38 the Bible says, "And Jesus cried with a loud voice, and gave up the ghost. And the veil of the temple was rent in twain from the top to the bottom" (KJV). When Jesus died, the veil was cut from top to bottom and that symbolizes that the way was now open for the human race to come before God. This is the reason why Jesus Christ is the way to God the Father. Through Jesus Christ we crossover.

The new and living way has been created for us through the veil and that veil refers to the body of Jesus

Christ. God is now building his church and the forces of evil cannot overcome it and the body of Christ is now that gateway to the Father.

This is what water baptism in the River Jordan for Jesus meant when John the Baptist baptized him. The baptism was declaring a clear message to the world that Jesus was going to die and then rise from the dead. This is how the way sweet fellowship between God and man would be restored. This is not just a religious tradition; it is a real life experience.

When people get baptized in water they are really proclaiming that they are identifying with Christ in his death and resurrection. This is the only way God has been speaking about for ages. No man can see God and still remain alive. In Christ, we die and resurrect so that we can see God. In Matthew 5:8 the Bible says, "Blessed are the pure in heart: for they shall see God" (KJV). Jesus is the way to God the Father.

Chapter 9
The Promise of the Father

God made a covenant with Abram and that led to the promise of giving him and his children land to occupy. In Genesis 15:12 -13 the Bible says, "And when the sun was going down, a deep sleep fell upon Abram; and, lo, an horror of great darkness fell upon him. And he said unto Abram, Know of a surety that thy seed shall be a stranger in a land that is not theirs, and shall serve them; and they shall afflict them four hundred years" (KJV). This was something that most people could have forgotten about, but the Hebrew people never forgot about it.

Moses wrote about it after it was talked about for generations. This was a promise of God, but later the promise became more than just a piece of land. The promise was really for the Holy Spirit from above.

Jesus talked about the promise of God the father with a special emphasis. This promise is more than what this world can offer or take away. The Lord blesses and adds no sorrow to his blessings. That is his plan for the human race. He wants us to know how to effectively defeat our enemy and that gives him pleasure.

The promise of God is not just a piece of land. It is the Spirit of God and he is the most precious gift in the whole wide world. The promise is not limited to a piece of land. It is not about things that are temporary. It is about the eternal blessings of God. The Holy Spirit means life forever, and when you have the Spirit of God you live forever. The blessing is not for a season because it is really for eternity.

When Jesus arose, he met with the disciples who confirmed that he was truly alive. He actually appeared to the disciples on different occasions for forty days before he ascended to the Father in heaven. On one occasion when Jesus met with the disciples he told them that he was sending them the promise of the Father which is the Holy Spirit. He wanted to make sure that they understood that he was sending them someone who would help them become effective at the task of reaching the human heart.

Jesus wanted the disciples to be equipped for the spiritual task that was ahead. The disciples had to be equipped for the mission. We are also supposed to be equipped for the same mission. They needed to be equipped the same way Jesus Christ was equipped when the Father sent him. We are supposed to be equipped the same way that is why Jesus said to the disciples that they should wait for the promise of the Father.

Now before Jesus ascended to the Father he reminded the disciples to wait for the promise of the Holy Spirit. After spending some time with the disciples for forty days, Jesus finally ascended to the Father. Ten days after he ascended to the Father, the Holy Spirit was poured out on the one hundred and twenty disciples who were waiting for the promise in the Upper room. When this happened, the disciples were changed from the inside. Now, when the disciples received the promise of the Father, the miracle working power was evident in their ministry.

Thousands of people got saved on that day of Pentecost alone after Peter preached about Jesus Christ. A few days later Peter and John were going to pray in the Temple according to Acts chapter three in the process felt compelled to help a disabled man. When both of them noticed that they had no money to give as arms to this disabled man, they instead commanded him to get up and walk. After pulling him by the hand his legs gained strength and he began to walk.

These disciples were now witnesses for Jesus because the Holy Spirit was working with them. In Mark 16: 20 the Bible declares, "And they went forth, and preached everywhere, the Lord working with them, and confirming the word with signs following. Amen" (KJV). The disciples now had power to convince the world that Jesus was the Son of God. They proved it to the people that Jesus was alive and well.

The Holy Spirit gives power to work miracles and has gifts that he manifests to build up his Church. In 1 Corinthians 12: 4 the Bible says, "Now there are diversities of gifts, but the same Spirit" (KJV). This means that the Holy Spirit manifests different gifts. These gifts do not belong to a human being. They do not belong to a single person. These are manifestations of the same Spirit of God to help build the church.

When believers gather together, the Holy Spirit manifests these gifts and those with spiritual needs receive the help they need. If someone needs healing, the Holy Spirit manifests the gift of healing. When someone needs salvation then the Holy Spirit would lead such a one to Jesus Christ. No one can come to God without the help of the Holy Spirit.

Chapter 10
The Kingdom of God

The kingdom of God is the kingdom of heaven. God is the king in heaven and he has sent his son to extend the same kingdom on earth.

In Matthew 4: 17 the Bible says, "From that time Jesus began to preach, and to say, Repent: for the kingdom of heaven is at hand" (KJV). Jesus came preaching the kingdom of God which would exert its power on earth as it does in heaven. When we pray, this is what we need to have in mind. We have to pray so that the will of God is done here on earth as it is done in heaven. Everyone in heaven obeys God. God is the King and what he wants done is what happens. The same thing is now being done here on earth because through Jesus Christ, God's kingdom has come.

Now, this kingdom of God is not like the kingdoms of this world. This kingdom does not come in ways of this world. How does it come? Well, the Bible in Mark 9: 1 says, "And he said unto them, Verily I say unto you, That there be some of them that stand here, which shall not taste of death, till they have seen the kingdom of God come with power" (KJV). The Kingdom of God comes with power.

When Jesus dealt with the skeptics he revealed the kingdom as being powerful. In Matthew 12: 28 the Bible says, "But if I cast out devils by the Spirit of God, then the kingdom of God is come unto you" (KJV). Demonic power has no part in the kingdom of God and Jesus demonstrated that by casting them out by the Spirit of God.

Whenever you are casting out demons in the name of Jesus please realize that it is done by the Spirit of God. The Spirit of God is the same Spirit of God in heaven and that same Spirit manifests the power of the Kingdom of God here on earth. God reigns here on earth by his Spirit. It is by his Spirit that we cast out demons. When we do this, it shows that the kingdom of God has now come to us.

What is the Kingdom of God? The Bible is clear on the subject and it says that it is not meat and drink. In Romans 14: 17 the Bible says, "For the kingdom of God is not meat and drink; but righteousness, and peace, and joy in the Holy Ghost" (KJV). The kingdom of God is about being right, having the peace of God and having joy, all by the Spirit of God. Jesus said that the kingdom of God is within us. In Luke 17:21 Jesus says, "Neither shall they say, Lo here! or, lo there! for, behold, the kingdom of God is within you" (KJV). The dynamics of

God's Kingdom are totally different from those of the kingdoms of men here on earth.

A natural eye can be mistaken if it searches for the kingdom of God by looking for characteristics that are known to establish the kingdoms of the world. The kingdom of God is not confined to a geographical location here on earth. It is in the hearts of those who believe in Jesus Christ. In the kingdom of God one important characteristic is power. It is all about you and I having power over sin which is only now possible through Jesus Christ. Surely the Kingdom of God has come.

When people receive Jesus Christ, they come into the kingdom of God. People in the kingdom of God are righteous and that righteousness is made possible because they believe in Jesus. This is the reason why the Bible clearly states that the unrighteousness will not inherit the kingdom of God. In 1 Corinthians 6:9 -10 the Bible says, "Know ye not that the unrighteous shall not inherit the kingdom of God? Be not deceived: neither fornicators, nor idolaters, nor adulterers, nor effeminate, nor abusers of themselves with mankind, Nor thieves, nor covetous, nor drunkards, nor revilers, nor extortioners, shall inherit the kingdom of God" (KJV). Sinners cannot inherit the kingdom of God. Only those who have faith in Christ are justified and ready to inherit the kingdom of God.

We are also told that flesh and blood cannot inherit the kingdom of God. Transformation must take place before those who believe in Christ can inherit the kingdom. In 1 Corinthians 15: 50 the Bible says, 'Now this I say, brethren, that flesh and blood cannot inherit the kingdom of God; neither doth corruption inherit incorruption" (KJV). What God has set out to do is to transform our bodies to be like the body that Christ has. Death had no power over his body.

In 1 Corinthians 15:53-54 the Bible says, "For this corruptible must put on incorruption, and this mortal must put on immortality. So when this corruptible shall have put on incorruption, and this mortal shall have put on immortality, then shall be brought to pass the saying that is written, Death is swallowed up in victory" (KJV). You and I must be transformed so that we can meet the body requirements for heaven. We must put on immortality because flesh and blood cannot inherit that kingdom.

Salvation from sin through Jesus Christ is the first step in the process of inheriting the kingdom of God. When we give our hearts to Jesus, we allow God as king to reign in our hearts. This allows the kingdom to be within us and through the authority of Christ we reign with him. In Luke 3:6 the Bible says, "And all flesh shall see the salvation of God" (KJV). The fact is that we shall reign with him in the world to come and that is why we now hope for that transformation.

In 1 Corinthians 15:52 the Bible says, "In a moment, in the twinkling of an eye, at the last trump: for the trumpet shall sound, and the dead shall be raised incorruptible, and we shall be changed" (KJV). We hope for that change because we shall be like Jesus Christ and death will not have power over us. This is how our bodies will inherit the kingdom of God. Our bodies will be changed by the power of God. This change is due to the fact that Jesus paid the price and that is why this will now happen to us. All we have to do now is to let him be our Lord and then just walk in obedience.

Obedience means taking desperate measures in our lives. Jesus taught the disciples to take desperate measures so as to enter the Kingdom of God. Entering the kingdom of God requires a complete separation from sin and Jesus Christ has made that possible for us. If anyone asks for forgive from God, he can find forgiveness no matter how sinful he might be. Jesus has the power to forgive anyone on earth.

In Matthew 7: 21 the Bible says, "Not every one that saith unto me, Lord, Lord, shall enter into the kingdom of heaven; but he that doeth the will of my Father which is in heaven" (KJV). Talking about the will of God is not enough, you have to do it. Practicing what the Bible teaches is a more obvious way of doing the will of God.

The will of God is something that stems from a relationship and it starts with a new birth experience. Only children of God can do the will of God therefore make sure you are saved. When you are saved, you enter the Kingdom of God. The kingdom is not just way in the by and by. You can enter the kingdom of God today.

What is the Kingdom of God? In Romans 14:17 the Bible says, "For the kingdom of God is not meat and drink; but righteousness, and peace, and joy in the Holy Ghost" (KJV). In the kingdom of God there is more than just physical food. It is also not just talk. In 1 Corinthians 4:20 the Scripture says, "For the kingdom of God is not with talk, but with power (KJV). The kingdom of God is full of activity. It is not as boring as many people might think. The kingdom of God involves a lot of action.

Jesus Christ teaches that we should take drastic measures to enter the Kingdom of God. That means action. In Mark 9:47 Jesus says, "And if thine eye offend thee, pluck it out: it is better for thee to enter into the kingdom of God with one eye, than having two eyes to be cast into hell fire" (KJV). Deal with whatever hinders you from entering the kingdom of God. A hindrance can also happen to be an idea, a sense of self sufficiency or hanging around with the wrong people. The word of God in 1 Corinthians 15, 33 says, "Be not deceived: evil communications corrupt good manners" (KJV). Take drastic measures for your life so that you can have peace with God.

Jesus considers having access into the kingdom more important than physical appeal. He allowed his body to be scarred for us. As a matter of fact, Jesus entered Heaven itself with nail scarred hands. He took drastic measures so that we can enter into the kingdom of God. If he did it for you and me it is then serious enough for us to take serious measures too. Whatever you do, make sure you enter into the Kingdom of God. Look at the opportunity cost, step out in faith and let nothing stop you!

In Luke 12:32 Jesus says, "Fear not, little flock; for it is your Father's good pleasure to give you the kingdom" (KJV). God delights in the fact that we come into his Kingdom. We are also supposed to proclaim our desire and appreciation for having God as our king. The Lord Jesus Christ teaches us that we should acknowledge God's kingdom in prayer. In Luke 6: 13 the lord Jesus teaches us to declare these words in prayer, "...For thine is the kingdom, and the power, and the glory, for ever. Amen" (KJV). It is comforting to note that God who is perfect in all his ways and full of mercy is King over us in his Kingdom.

A king has a lot of power in a kingdom and if a king is a man with all his natural sinful passions, he can end up being destructive. The people he governs can end up suffering because of his misuse of power. There is no one who is perfectly suited for being a king except God. God is perfect in all his ways and his judgments are right. Rejecting God as King is like rejecting life and all its blessings.

At one time the nation of Israel rejected God as King and that is why in 1 Samuel 8:4-5 the Bible says, "Then all the elders of Israel gathered themselves together, and came to Samuel unto Ramah, And said unto him, Behold, thou art old, and thy sons walk not in thy ways: now make us a king to judge us like all the nations" (KJV). Samuel the prophet knew very well what all this was leading to.

At first, he thought the people were rejecting him as a prophet. However, he later learnt that the people were really rejected God as there king. This also implied that they would end up suffering under the leadership of a man with all his evil passions. Samuel knew that such a man would misuse his power as a king. They rejected God who was full of compassion and that was a sad situation.

The Lord clearly stated that the people were really rejecting God as their king. In 1 Samuel 8: 7 the Bible says, "And the Lord said unto Samuel, Hearken unto the voice of the people in all that they say unto thee: for they have not rejected thee, but they have rejected me, that I should not reign over them" (KJV). Although Samuel misunderstood the situation because he thought the people were rejecting him, the Lord clearly showed him that the people were really rejecting God as their king.

When we preach the gospel the message we share poses a challenge before the people to either accept or reject God. When they do not accept Jesus, it means they are rejecting God. As a matter of fact, they are rejecting God as King over their lives. When repentance is preached, it means the kingdom of God is near. Right now, the kingdom of God is being preached and the people who accept Jesus Christ as Lord and Savior enter into the kingdom that God has established.

The kingdom of God is a kingdom that can never be overthrown. That is why in Hebrews 1: 8 in reference to Jesus the Bible says, "But unto the Son he saith, Thy throne, O God, is for ever and ever: a sceptre of righteousness is the sceptre of thy kingdom" (KJV). Jesus is King and he holds a sceptre of righteousness in his hand and that sceptre signals what he wants done in his kingdom.

God's judgments are righteous at all times. All you need is faith in Jesus Christ to enter God's Kingdom and be able to receive his promises. Step out in faith and crossover to life. Now is your time.